SPEND MORE MONEY
in
RETIREMENT

It May be More than You Think

A Workbook

James Schweinsburg

Copyright and Disclaimer

Acknowledgments

Putting into words and on paper, the many things I have learned in preparing for and living in retirement, was both rewarding and exhausting. This workbook would not have come to be without the encouragement and support of my loving wife of 50 years Cecilia.

I would like to give a special thanks to those that helped make this workbook better. To Steve Schenck, a scientist, whose pickiness and thoroughness made this workbook more readable and understandable. To Brad Valentine, an executive nearing retirement, whose enthusiasm for the workbook's subject matter, encouragement, and feedback gave me the courage to publish this workbook. To Sharon Sabelhaus, recently retired, who is learning about retirement finances and working with a financial planner, provided valuable insight and perspective as she tried to learn from the workbook.

Table of Contents

Introduction

This workbook is the culmination of searching several years for the answer to one of the most important retirement questions; ***How much can I safely spend in retirement each year?*** This led me to seek the answer to another critical question; ***If I need or want to spend more than my retirement income, how much of my savings can I safely withdraw each year so that I do not outlive my savings?*** The answers to these questions are provided by this workbook.

Why is this book different from the many books written on this subject? First, I am not a professional Financial Planner or Investment Adviser. I am a retired executive and engineer, trained and experienced in analyzing and solving difficult problems. I have learned many lessons in preparing for, and living in retirement for several years, which I believe allows me to bring a fresh perspective and simplification to this complex subject.

Second, it is a workbook that guides you step by step through the process of selecting an appropriate retirement savings withdrawal system, and then helps you determine the amount that you can safely spend in retirement each year. It is not just another retirement planning book that explains all the complexities of the issues facing retirees, explains their advantages and disadvantages, but then leaves you without an actual executable plan.

Third, this workbook will not try to get you to buy additional services or publications like many financial books and authors attempt to do. This workbook was written to share what I have learned in planning for retirement and what I have learned since retiring. The hope is that you find this workbook of value in planning your retirement.

The name for this workbook was chosen after reading about how many retirees underspend in retirement possibly depriving themselves of a more enjoyable retirement. There are many reasons for this, maybe some psychological and some behavioral, but not knowing how much can be safely spent without outliving retirement savings, is a significant obstacle.

No retirement spending and savings withdrawal system is perfect, and all have their advantages and disadvantages. This workbook explains and compares four popular but completely different withdrawal systems that many financial planners have suggested to their clients.

The four withdrawal systems chosen for consideration in this workbook are the 4% Withdrawal system, the 1/N Withdrawal system, the IRS Required Minimum Distribution (RMD) Withdrawal system, and the Variable Percentage Withdrawal (VPW) system. These are explained in detail in Chapter 3. This workbook will guide you in choosing which of the four withdrawal systems you are most comfortable with.

Left out of this workbook is the withdrawal strategy that suggest you only spend the interest and dividends your investments generate each year and not touch the principal. Very few of us have the wealth necessary for this strategy to provide a satisfying lifestyle in retirement.

Long before thinking about writing this workbook, I researched many different savings withdrawal systems and created a computerized spreadsheet program to help me plan for my retirement and help me organize my thoughts. I wanted a computer program that allowed me to calculate the effects of a variety of what-if scenarios and help me choose a savings withdrawal system that I would be most comfortable with. I wanted a program that could analyze various spending budgets, determine how much could be safely withdrawn from available savings (without running out of money under various time horizons), and help track progress.

The current version of the spreadsheet program, which is the basis of this workbook, is available for free when you purchase this workbook. It includes the necessary worksheets and automates much of the data input and number crunching, saving you time. It has gone through many revisions and improvements in the years since it was created.

For those of you who are familiar with computer spreadsheets, I urge you to get It before you start using the worksheets in Chapter 7. For those of you not familiar with spreadsheets, I created a computer file containing all the worksheets so you can print them out and use them each year. See the Afterword section at the end of the workbook on how to get them.

This workbook is organized around the logical steps to building a successful retirement. It will help you to:

1. Create your retirement plan.

2. Create the retirement Lifestyle you want.

3. Choose a savings withdrawal system you are most comfortable with.

4. Navigate the many risks you may face in retirement.

5. Decide what savings and investment accounts to withdraw from and in what order to minimize taxes and maximize investment returns.

6. Decide where to invest for safety, diversification, growth and peace of mind.

Although the main focus of this workbook is to help you determine what retirement lifestyle you can afford and help you select a savings withdrawal system that is designed to help prevent you from outliving your savings, I have expanded it to include additional topics that I have found to be important in building a successful retirement plan.

- **8** -

You cannot predict the future with certainty, but this workbook will help you make the decisions and calculations you need to make in order to determine if your planned lifestyle is achievable. If you choose to work with a financial planner hopefully this workbook will provide you with valuable information.

CAUTION: The future may contain scenarios that are better or worse than anything considered by this workbook. It is also important to remember that, despite the sophistication of the methods used, this workbook makes several simplifying assumptions. Note that the Suggested Withdrawal amounts are just that, Suggestions, and are designed to prevent you from significantly over or under spending your savings. It is highly recommended that you seek additional guidance in developing a retirement plan with which you will be most comfortable.

Chapter *1*

Create Your Retirement Plan

Creating a retirement spending & investing plan requires, among other things:

- Estimating how long you will live.

- Creating a spending budget that supports your retirement lifestyle.

- Understanding the trade-off between spending money in the early years of retirement against saving money for your later years.

- Choosing how much to invest in stocks, bonds and cash for safety, diversification, and hopefully investment growth to protect against inflation.

- Deciding when to take Social Security benefits.

- Understanding how taxes in retirement will reduce your income.

Your retirement plan also needs to be able to manage the risks of running out of money or having to significantly reduce your retirement lifestyle in the latter years of your retirement. There are three major risks that cannot be known:

- **Longevity risk** is not knowing how long you will live.

- **Market risk** is the possibility that poor market returns will significantly reduce or deplete your spendable investments too soon and thus produce a less than desirable retirement.

- **Unexpected spending risk** or major unplanned expenses such as major health expenses, that can reduce the available savings that were being counted on for an enjoyable retirement.

How long do you want your plan to last?

More specifically, how long do you want your savings to last to support your retirement plan. If you and/or your partner are reasonably healthy, a safe age to use is 95, with 100 not unreasonable with the advances being made in medicine Today. Depending on what life expectancy table or study you use, a reasonably healthy 65-year-old male on average will live to age 88 and has a 10 to 20% chance of making it to age 95. A reasonably healthy female can expect to live about 2.5 years longer.

The longevity of an opposite sex couple in reasonably good health, increases the chances of one of you making it to age 95 to 20 to 40%. Since there is better than a 10% chance of living to 95, it is a reasonable, conservative and less risky age to use.

The calculations in this workbook are limited to a maximum of 38 years of withdrawals so if you are 62 at the beginning of the first year in retirement you could enter an ending age up to age 100, if you want your savings to last that long. Obviously the longer you want your savings to last the less you can withdraw each year. Conversely, the risk of outliving your savings goes up as you shorten the length.

How will your spending change with age?

Popular belief is that your spending will increase as you age due to inflation and the rising costs of health care, but some studies suggest otherwise. Data from the Bureau of Labor Statistics suggests the opposite is true. It shows that spending tends to peak at age 55 and then for every 10 years after it drops approximately 10 to 14%. Although healthcare expenses nearly double during

- 11 -

this period, almost all other expenses steadily decline. The big question mark is the amount of travel expenses incurred in the first few years of retirement when you have newfound time on your hands and a bucket list you want to pursue.

When thinking about retirement possibly lasting 30 or more years, I believe, as many financial planners do, that there are three retirement phases that most retirees will go through. I like to call them;

- **The Bucket List phase** when you are most active with newfound time on your hands and lots of things you want to do.

- **The Let's Relax phase** where you have completed most of your bucket list and are physically starting to slow down.

- **Homebound phase** where most discretionary expenses disappear, and your largest expense may be medical. The age that each phase starts and ends of course is dependent to a large extent on the retiree's health.

When to take Social Security Benefits?

Many financial planners recommend delaying receiving Social Security benefits until your 70th birthday. The reason is that for every year you postpone your benefits, they will be increased 8% until age 70. That's a 32% increase above your eligible benefit at 66 and 76% above you're benefit at 62. And remember that the increases are for the remainder of your life. Plus, the annual cost of living increases, are calculated as a percentage of the previous year's benefits, so the compounding of those increases over the length of your retirement can be large.

A recent study by Massachusetts Mutual Life Insurance Company found that almost 40% of retirees regretted taking Social Security benefits early. They also found that even using the most conservative cumulative calculation, a married couple living into their early 90's could be forfeiting more than

$500,000 or as much as $2000 to $4000 per month for life, by filing for Social Security benefits at age 62 versus age 70. The study also found that a surviving spouse could receive $1000 to $2000 per month less as a result of filing at 62.

Think of delaying social security as buying one of the best annuities plans you can get, paid for with the benefit money you would have received. As an example, delaying benefits four years, from age 66 to 70 years old, is like an annuity that pays for itself in about 13 to 16 years, or by the age of 83 to 86, based on the significant increase in benefit payments starting at age 70. In addition, the higher benefit amounts received beyond the break-even point will be at a time when they're often needed the most.

Note that the break-even point for recouping the value of delayed benefits is not a simple calculation since it is affected by inflation rates and by portfolio growth rates. Depending on if and how much of the early benefit payments are invested, or allows existing savings to not be spent, will allow the amount to grow longer. The lower the growth rate, the shorter the break-even period, because invested early withdrawals will grow slower. Also, the higher the inflation rate, the shorter the break-even period, because future higher benefit payments will compound faster with larger cost of living adjustments.

While your situation may not appear to allow you to delay receiving benefits, depending on your income and spending needs, it may make sense to tap other sources of income first such as:

- Some studies suggest that it may be advantageous for the lower earning spouse to take benefits early and the higher earning spouse to delay until age 70.

- Working part time at your old job, if that is a possibility, or other part-time work while in your 60s that pays an amount nearly equal to your monthly benefit if you took Social Security early.

- Maybe tap your savings that may only be earning 1-2% interest if you have more than needed for an emergency. Should avoid selling investments that have growth potential.

- 13 -

- Depending on your income tax bracket it may make sense to withdraw from your 401K or IRA.

If you use other sources to make up for delayed Social Security benefits, your goal should be to keep the withdrawals as low as possible. *I strongly advise you seek additional information on this extremely important decision.*

The Income Tax Surprise!

Many retirees believe that their taxes will go down once they retire and will become simpler, but I have found the opposite to be true. The biggest surprise was the income tax on Social Security benefits, due to IRA withdrawals, Capital gains, and income from part time work that can easily increase income well above the threshold for taxes to be paid on benefits.

The tax is not easy to calculate, and is beyond the scope of this workbook, but as an example, for the 2019 tax year, a married couple filing jointly, will pay taxes on up to 50% of their Social Security income if their combined income is $32,000 to $44,000. If more than $44,000, they can expect to pay taxes on up to 85% of their Social Security benefits. The IRS considers combined income as including one-half of your social security income, so it does not take much additional income before you start paying taxes on part of your social security income.

Another surprise was computing the income tax got more complicated in retirement and having to make quarterly estimated income taxes if you expect to owe more than $1000 that are not paid through withholding. These complications, especially avoiding penalties, may require you to consult with a tax professional.

The following chapters will help you continue to build a sustainable retirement plan, one that hopefully provides for a rewarding retirement.

Chapter *2*

Create your Retirement Lifestyle

The First Step is to determine the retirement lifestyle you hope your income and savings can support over your entire retirement. Creating a realistic spending budget is critical in developing a retirement plan that does not run out of money before you run out of time. This workbook will guide you in creating your desired spending budget if you do not already have a budgeting system.

This workbook assumes you already have a general idea of the lifestyle you want in retirement, and a good understanding of how your financial situation may change once you stop working. Consider how the three phases of retirement spending, mentioned in the first chapter, may affect your retirement plan. If you are still working fulltime it is important to consider how you will spend all your free time when you retire.

Many retirees underestimate the void created when they stop working. Although it is an exciting time, it's also a time of drastic change. While it might seem like fun at first, after a few years, it could become more difficult to find ways to fill your days. Many retirees, including myself, found easing into retirement over several years reduced the shock of going from working 40 plus hours per week to zero.

If you have not spent enough time and effort in understanding how your income and expenses will change as you enter retirement, Appendix I provides a list of things to consider in creating your retirement lifestyle. The success of your retirement depends on having a well thought out plan. It does not need to be too detailed at first so long as you continue to add detail and create as realistic a plan as possible.

This workbook also assumes you want to spend most if not all your savings & investments by the length you choose for it to last. If you want to leave money to your heirs, and/or you want some extra measure of safety, this workbook provides for this as well, and you can see the effect those decisions have.

Hopefully you already have a spending budget prior to retiring from which to start from. Chapter 7 Worksheet 1 is where you will create your desired spending budget. If you already have a budgeting system that you prefer to use, you can simply enter the total annual estimated spending amount in the appropriate Withdrawals Worksheet that is selected in Chapter 7. I highly recommend using a budgeting program or App to simplify the creation and tracking of actual expenses compared to the budgeted amounts.

As you will see later in this workbook, it is very desirable to separate your budget into *Needs* and *Wants* to determine the amount of flexibility your spending will have. Spending flexibility especially early in your retirement can be helpful if you must adjust your spending budget for a series of possible investment down years. Regardless, keeping fixed and essential expenses as low as possible will not only increase spending flexibility, but during investment up years may allow you to spend more than you might think on the enjoyable parts of your retirement.

If this is your first attempt at a detailed budget think Big Picture first, then add details as you go. The goal is to create as realistic a spending budget as possible. Keeping track and recording what was spent each month will help you see how realistic your budget is, help identify where you might be able to adjust your spending and help improve accuracy over time.

The Second Step is to identify your sources of retirement income. This will be subtracted from your desired spending budget to arrive at the amount you may need to withdraw from savings to support your desired lifestyle. Chapter 7 Worksheet 2 is where you will enter your estimated income for the current year, and it should be done at the beginning of each year in retirement.

You will also need to estimate income taxes on income, interest, dividends and taxes on withdrawing from your tax deferred investments like 401k or IRA distributions. This may include income taxes on your Social Security benefits. Again, think Big Picture first then add details as you go. Keeping track and recording income received each month will help improve accuracy over time.

The Third Step is to estimate the total savings & investments available to be withdrawn over the length of your retirement to support your desired lifestyle. For simplicity I use the term Portfolio interchangeably with available savings and investments.

Chapter 7 Worksheet 3 is where to determine the total value of your portfolio that is available for you to spend in retirement. It should not include the value of Life Insurance, Home, Auto or other personal items that may be difficult to convert into spending. Also, it should not include the value of any annuities whose payments should be included in income.

The worksheet will allow you to allocate money for an Emergency Fund, any money you want to leave to your heirs, and any money to be used as a cushion for the later years of retirement or in case you or your spouse live longer than your plan allowed. These are then subtracted from the total to determine the spendable portion of your portfolio. This amount is used in the appropriate Savings Withdrawals Worksheet to determine the suggested annual withdrawal amount.

Unexpected major expenses happen, so money should be set aside for these unplanned non budgeted expenses. If your income sources are mostly guaranteed then the emergency fund only needs to cover the expense and not lost wages, so it can be much lower than during your working years.

The Fourth Step is to choose a retirement withdrawal system that you are most comfortable with. This is probably the hardest and most important decision you will need to make in order to create a successful retirement spending and withdrawal plan.

Once you select a savings withdrawal system, the appropriate worksheet in Chapter 7 will calculate the Safe Withdrawal Amount. It will also determine what adjustments may need to be made to your planned lifestyle based upon the suggested safe annual spending amounts.

The next chapter explains in detail the four very different retirement withdrawal systems that have been recommended by many financial planners and publications. Chapter 4 will compare the withdrawal systems and explain the advantages and disadvantages of each system, so you can decide which fits your retirement plan the best.

Chapter *3*

Choose a Savings Withdrawal System

The goal is to make your savings last as long as you do so that you can continue to live comfortably in the latter years of retirement. There are many retirement savings withdrawal systems that have been created and studied over the years. They are all designed to make your savings last as long as you do while attempting to manage the risks of failure.

After having studied many different withdrawal systems, I chose what I believe are the four most often recommended and thoroughly tested savings withdrawal systems in use today. They each have advantages and disadvantages and are impacted differently by the amount of investment gains, inflation rates, and the Portfolio allocation of Stocks to Bonds to Cash. The impact of these variables is discussed in more detail in this chapter and the following chapter. For a reference to the historical financial performance over the last 90 years see Appendix II Table 5A.

A common issue when using a typical retirement savings withdrawal system is that the suggested withdrawal percentage is usually based on a worst-case scenario. That is, the recommended percentage is one that, in the past, would have allowed you to weather the worst stock market down period in the last 50 to 90 years, if it occurs again during your retirement. While it is considered safe to assume the worst, what often happens during retirement is that the markets perform better than the worst-case scenario. The four withdrawal systems that follow, all assume worst case or near worst case scenarios when testing or back testing the results with historical data.

The 4% Withdrawal System: This system known as the 4% Rule is probably the most recognized, and until recent years, was among the most widely used withdrawal system. It is simple to apply based on how long you would like your savings to last. Many Financial Planners have recommended this system based on a groundbreaking study published in 1994 by Bengen. The original study suggested that 4% would be a safe withdrawal percent to use at the start of a 30-year retirement based on a worst-case scenario using historical data and having a 95% probability of success.

At the start of your retirement, simply enter how long you would like your savings to last and this Workbook uses a table to determine the starting withdrawal amount. At the start of a 38-year retirement, for example, it uses a 3.4 % withdrawal rate to arrive at a starting withdrawal amount during the first year of retirement. You then increase that amount each year by the previous year inflation rate.

If you started your retirement later in life and wanted your retirement to last 25 years, it uses a 4.7% starting withdrawal rate. The simplicity of this system is that regardless of how your investments perform in subsequent years you just withdraw the previous year's amount and increase it by the previous year inflation rate. It provides a stable annual spending amount that only varies by the inflation rate.

The inflation rate has a significant effect on withdrawals over time, and therefore, how long your savings will last. The annual inflation rate has averaged 2.6% over the last 30 years and 3.6% over the last 40 years. If, however the previous year's inflation rate is higher than 3% I suggest you should limit the annual adjustment for inflation to be 3% max and adjust your spending. This should lower your withdrawal amount slightly to prevent the possibility of running out of money later in retirement due to inflation averaging higher than 3%.

Also, the average annual gain of your portfolio over the course of your retirement will have a significant affect. Some studies suggest the 4% starting withdrawal rate at the start of a 30 plus year retirement is too high based on

- 20 -

the expectation that future investment gains will average less than the historical average. However, those studies were based on worst case scenarios and other studies have shown that most of the time a starting withdrawal rate of 4.0% is very conservative over a 30-year retirement. Appendix II Table 5A lists historical financial data including inflation rates of the last 50 years and how the stock and Bond markets have performed.

Although the 4% system provides short-term spending stability, the major disadvantage of the 4% system, and the reason this system is falling out of favor with many financial planners, is that the long-term effect on the portfolio is unpredictable. One of the reasons is, it does not allow a reduction in withdrawals if your investments perform poorly over the course of your entire retirement horizon, and thus **It Does Not Prevent You from Running Out of Money Earlier Than Planned.**

Without adjusting annual withdrawal amounts based on how your investments are performing, your investments could grow slowly over time to a significant amount which would be left unspent during your retirement. If your investments perform poorly over an extended period, it could also be depleted before you had planned on.

Remember that the basis for the 4% system is that the starting withdrawal amount once determined does not change from year to year except for inflation adjustments. It assumes future investment gains and losses over the course of your retirement will perform similar to the worst-case historical performance. The impact that inflation rates and average portfolio gains have on your retirement are discussed in Chapter 4.

Even if you decide against using this withdrawal system, it at least provides a conservative rule of thumb in determining how much savings and investments you may need to retire. You estimate your desired annual spending amount to achieve the lifestyle you want, then subtract your estimated after-tax retirement income, and then divide that amount by 4% (or multiply it by 25) to arrive at the amount of savings and investments you may need at the start of your retirement.

The 1/N Withdrawal System: One method to allow spending more money from your savings during the years you expect to draw from it is to spend a percentage calculated based on the remaining years left in retirement. This ensures that your savings will last the length of time you choose.

In the 1/N withdrawal method, the 'N' is equal to the number of years remaining between your current age and the age you have chosen for your savings to be depleted. The worksheet determines this number and it is recalculated each year because you have one less year remaining. This results in a higher percentage being withdrawn from the portfolio each year.

As an example, if you are currently 71 at the beginning of the year and you want your savings to last until age 95 you have 24 years of withdrawals remaining. You then determine your available portfolio value at the end of the previous year and divide this by 24 to determine the amount you can withdraw this year. The next year you would have 23 years remaining, so you divide the available portfolio value by 23 to determine your withdrawal amount, and so on.

Notice that each year you are dividing your portfolio by a smaller number which translates to an increasing percentage each year. Normally, withdrawing a higher percentage each year is considered possibly unsafe, as it may result in the portfolio being eventually depleted. However, using a 1/N withdrawal method typically assumes spending most, if not all the portfolio, so large withdrawal percentages near the end of your retirement are not a concern. If you had 2 years to live, then what would a 'safe' withdrawal percentage be? Since you know the portfolio must only last two years you could safely withdraw 50% of the portfolio.

The advantage of this system is that you cannot outlive your savings unless you live beyond the years you chose for your savings to last. A possible disadvantage of the 1/N strategy is that it suggests a withdrawal amount that is much less in the early years of retirement and much more in the later years. Some studies have shown that you may spend less as you age, especially if you are in reasonably good health or have good medical insurance. What if you want to spend more in the early stages of retirement when you are more active with hobby and travel expenses.

Another possible disadvantage of the 1/N strategy is the amount you withdraw each year will vary with how well your investments did the previous year, so in a significant down year you may have to significantly reduce spending. This will require that you have a flexible spending budget with significant discretionary expenses that can be reduced. As an example, a 20% stock market down year could result in your portfolio being down 20% or more which could result in you having to reduce spending by 20% or more than the amount you spent in the previous year.

To reduce the possible swings in spending from year to year, some adviser's suggest setting limits on how much you need to reduce spending and cap how much more you can spend in good years. See Chapter 6 for details on how this can affect the success of your plan and smooth out year to year withdrawal variability.

The 1/N strategy's annual withdrawal % is not affected by inflation or the average annual portfolio gain because the withdrawal amount it suggests you take uses the actual portfolio value at the end of the previous year and assumes your spending budget for the coming year already has been adjusted for expected spending changes, which should include changes based on increases due to inflation.

The RMD Withdrawal System: This system is based on a table created by the IRS to determine the Required Minimum Distribution from tax advantage accounts like 401K and traditional IRA's. It is based on life expectancy tables. Even if you do not have any tax advantage accounts the theory behind the table can still apply and some financial planners recommend this system as a conservative withdrawal system for retirees.

The Lookup Table used in this workbook was adjusted from a starting age of 70 used by the IRS table, to a starting age of 62 and is based on the same life expectancy tables used by the IRS RMD. The table then converts the percentages to divisors to make the calculation simpler.

The RMD withdrawal system is easy to apply and allows the withdrawal percentage to increase each year as your remaining life expectancy decreases. You take the value of your portfolio at the end of the previous year then divide it by the number that you look up in the RMD withdrawal table based on your age at the beginning of the year.

Like the 1/N withdrawal system a potential disadvantage is the amount you withdraw each year will vary with how well your portfolio did the previous year. See Chapter 6 for details on how you might be able to smooth out year-to-year withdrawal variability.

Also, like the 1/N strategy the annual withdrawal % is not affected by inflation or the average annual portfolio gain because the suggested withdrawal amount uses the actual portfolio value at the end of the previous year and assumes your spending budget is adjusted for real inflation each year.

The advantage of this system is that you cannot outlive your savings. However, it is not designed to deplete your savings at the end of the age you choose like the 1/N and VPW withdrawal systems, because even at age 95 at the beginning of the year, it suggests a withdrawal rate of 12.4%. Due to its conservative withdrawals in the later years of retirement it most likely will leave money in your portfolio which depending on how well your investment gains did, could be a significant amount that you could have spent during retirement.

<u>The Variable Percentage Withdrawal System:</u> Known simply as the VPW withdrawal system, this is a withdrawal method that adjusts to retirement length, asset allocation, and investment returns during retirement. It attempts to combine the best ideas of the constant-dollar, constant-percentage, and 1/N systems to allow you to spend your savings using withdrawals that have been adjusted by market returns. By adjusting your withdrawal amounts based on how well your portfolio did the previous year, it is designed like the 1/N and RMD systems so you cannot outlive your savings unless you live beyond the years you chose for your savings to last.

The VPW withdrawal system is easy to apply and allows the withdrawal percentage to increase each year as your remaining life expectancy decreases. You take the value of your portfolio at the end of the previous year and then multiply it by the suggested withdrawal % that you look up in the VPW withdrawal table based on the years remaining in your plan and the stock to bond percentage reflected in your portfolio. You can select between a conservative ratio of 20/80, a moderate 40/60, a more aggressive 60/40, or a very aggressive 80/20.

Higher stock ratios should result in improved portfolio performance over the length of your retirement, but at higher risk, so the withdrawal % it suggests reflects this. See Appendix II Table 5B for the impact that the years remaining and stock to bond ratios have on the VPW withdrawal percentages.

Like the 1/N and RMD withdrawal methods a possible disadvantage of the VPW withdrawal system is your annual withdrawal amounts will always fluctuate with your year-end investment values. As with the 1/N and RMD systems setting limits on how much you can reduce spending and cap how much more you can spend in good years will reduce spending variability. See Chapter 6 for more details on how this can affect the success of your plan and smooth out year-to-year withdrawal variability.

The VPW method and suggested withdrawal rates were collaboratively developed and improved by a group of Bogleheads®. I highly recommend going to their website www.bogleheads.org for much more information.

Chapter *4*

Compare Withdrawal Systems

In this chapter we will compare the effects that the four savings withdrawal systems have on a hypothetical 65-year-old starting retirement with a total spendable portfolio of $500,000 and wanting the portfolio to last until age 95, or 30 years of withdrawals. It compares a 3% average annual inflation to a 4% annual inflation rate for the 4% withdrawal system, which is the only withdrawal system impacted by the inflation rate. It compares a 20/80, 40/60, and 60/40 stock to bond investment ratios for the VPW system which is the only withdrawal system that uses different withdrawal rates based on the stock to bond ratio. It will also show the impact that an average annual investment gain of 3.5%, 4.5%, 5.5%, and 6.5% will have over 30 years on all four withdrawal systems.

This comparison is for illustrative purposes only and represents a summary of the results that were generated using a spreadsheet program that I developed several years ago to do What-If comparisons of the four withdrawal systems. It is important to note that the program assumes that the average annual gains studied average that amount every year in retirement, but of course we know this doesn't happen in real life. The sequence in which the annual gains or losses occur can have a dramatic effect on your retirement plan and the results presented in this chapter. The impact that this sequence of investment gains or losses, known as "Sequence of returns," risk, has on the success of your retirement lifestyle is discussed in the next chapter.

I believe the analysis presented in this chapter is useful in illustrating the differences that the four withdrawal systems have under the same set of assumptions. See Appendix II Table 5B for the annual withdrawal percentages used for each of the withdrawal systems. See the Afterword section at the end of the workbook if you are interested in obtaining the spreadsheet program to analyze your own retirement plan.

Total withdrawn over 30 years:

Table 1A shows how much each system would withdraw over the entire 30-year period under differing average annual portfolio gains. Notice that the 1/N withdrawal system results in the largest total amount withdrawn over 30 years. This is because the 1/N system withdraws a significantly less amount in the early years of retirement, as shown in table 1C, compared to the other systems and thus allows for a larger portfolio balance to grow over time.

The VPW system is impacted by the stock to bond ratio which affects total average annual portfolio gains. As the stock to bond ratio increases, the average portfolio gains over 30 years should increase as well but of course with more risk. The program automatically adjusts the average gain that is input to reflect the historical differences in various stock to bond ratios. For comparison purposes I show the impact that a 20/80,40/60, and 60/40 ratio would have on total withdrawals over 30 years. As can be seen, the 40/60 and 60/40 ratios withdraw the second most amount next to the 1/N system.

Notice the RMD withdrawal system withdraws significantly less over the entire retirement withdrawal period compared to the 1/N because its withdrawals are much more conservative in the later years, and it most likely will leave a considerable amount at the end of your retirement as Table 1B shows.

Notice that the 4% Withdrawal system's total withdrawals peak at $970,000 with a 3% annual inflation rate and peaks at $1,144,000 with a 4% annual inflation rate. This is because the amount drawn each year is only adjusted for the inflation rate, so unless it runs out of money early due to poor annual portfolio gains, it peaks at 30 years, in this example, if the average annual portfolio gain is 4.5%. With a 4% annual inflation rate it peaks with a 5.6% or higher average annual portfolio gain.

- 27 -

Portfolio value after 30 years:

Table 1B looks at what the $500,000 portfolio at the start of a 30-year retirement would be at the end of 30 years, for each of the four withdrawal systems, under differing average annual gains. The 4% withdrawal system in table 1B shows that it is significantly impacted by how the portfolio performs over time and the inflation rate. This could result in either running out of savings earlier than planned or end up with a significant portfolio value after 30 years.

As an example, Table 1B shows that if the 4% withdrawal system averages a 3.5% average annual portfolio gain over 30 years, which is worst case, and the inflation rate averages 3%, you could run out of money by age 91, or 4 years earlier than planned. If the inflation rate averages 4%, you could run out of money by age 88, or 7 years earlier. If it averages an annual 4.5% portfolio gain and the inflation rate is 4%, you could also run out of money by age 91. However, if both inflation and the average annual portfolio gain is near historical averages of 3% inflation and 6.5% gains, you could end up with $665,000 that you were not able to spend for a more enjoyable retirement!

Notice that the 1/N, RMD, and VPW withdrawal systems, regardless of investment performance, never run out of money over the length of time you chose for your savings to last. However, the suggested annual withdrawal amount is based on the value of your portfolio at the end of the previous year so depending on how well your investments performed, you may have had to significantly reduce withdrawals and spending during portfolio down years.

Note that the RMD withdrawal system like the 4% withdrawal system, is not designed to deplete your savings at the end of the age you choose like the 1/N and VPW withdrawal systems. This is because even at age 95 at the beginning of the year, the RMD withdrawal system suggests a withdrawal rate of only 12.4%. Due to its conservative withdrawals in the later years of retirement, most likely it will leave a significant amount that could have been spent during retirement.

- 28 -

Withdrawals in the early years versus later years:

Table 1C compares the amount withdrawn during the first 10 years of retirement to the amount withdrawn in the last 10 years of a 30-year retirement, for each of the four withdrawal systems under differing average annual gains. The VPW withdrawal system withdraws the most in the first 10 years of retirement because the withdrawal percentages that it suggests are higher at the start of retirement than the other systems. However, because it withdraws more money early, your portfolio depletes slightly faster and thus will grow more slowly over time.

The 4% withdrawal system is designed to withdraw the same amount regardless of how much your portfolio gains, but as you can see, at a low average annual gain of 3.5% it runs out of money before 30 years, which reduces the amount available in the last 10 years of retirement. The 1/N withdrawal system withdraws the least in the first 10 years but by far the most in the last 10 years. As previously mentioned, it has the lowest starting withdrawal percentages and the highest in the later years.

If we look at the amount withdrawn in the first 10 years compared to the last 10 years, as a percent of the total withdrawn over 30 years, and using a 3% inflation rate and 5.5% average annual portfolio gain, the 4% withdrawal system withdraws 24% of the total in the first 10 years and 44% in the last 10 years, the 1/N system withdraws 18% and 52% respectively, the RMD system withdraws 21% and 45% respectively, and the VPW system withdraws 26% and 41% respectively with a 40/60 stock to bond ratio.

Keep in mind that the program used to create the following comparison tables did not do multiple simulations using various sequences of portfolio gains or losses. It is simply comparing results under one set of assumptions.

Table 1A

Avg Annual Gain	Total withdrawn after 30 years starting with $500,000						
	4% System		1/N System	RMD System	VPW System		
	3% Inflation	4% Inflation			20/80	40/60	60/40
3.50%	$787,000	$758,000	**$860,000**	$706,000	$752,000	$796,000	$832,000
4.50%	$970,000	$904,000	**$1,017,000**	$825,000	$853,000	$920,000	$978,000
5.50%	$970,000	$1,139,000	**$1,207,000**	$969,000	$972,000	$1,071,000	$1,157,000
6.50%	$970,000	$1,144,000	**$1,439,000**	$1,143,000	$1,111,000	$1,252,000	$1,379,000

Table 1B

Avg Annual Gain	Portfolio value after 30 years starting with $500,000						
	4% System		1/N System	RMD System	VPW System		
	3% Inflation	4% Inflation			20/80	40/60	60/40
3.50%	**$0 after 26 yrs.**	**$0 after 23 yrs.**	$0	$200,000	$0	$0	$0
4.50%	**$0 after 30 yrs.**	**$0 after 26 yrs.**	$0	$264,000	$0	$0	$0
5.50%	$276,000	$0	$0	$348,000	$0	$0	$0
6.50%	$665,000	$355,000	$0	$458,000	$0	$0	$0

- 30 -

Table 1C

First 10 years withdrawals compared to last 10 years of a 30 year retirement									

	4% System				1/N System		RMD System		
Avg.	3% Annual Inflation		4% Annual Inflation						
Annual	First	Last	First	Last	First	Last	First	Last	
Gain	10 years	10 years	10 years	10 years	10 years	10 years	10 years	10 years	
3.50%	$234,000	$239,000	$245,000	$151,000	$195,000	$389,000	$186,000	$275,000	
4.50%	$234,000	$422,000	$245,000	$297,000	$205,000	$494,000	$194,000	$348,000	
5.50%	$234,000	$422,000	$245,000	$532,000	$214,000	$626,000	$204,000	$440,000	
6.50%	$234,000	$422,000	$245,000	$536,000	$225,000	$792,000	$213,000	$556,000	

	VPW System					
Avg.	20/80		40/60		60/40	
Annual	First	Last	First	Last	First	Last
Gain	10 years	10 years	10 years	10 years	10 years	10 years
3.50%	$238,000	$263,000	$255,000	$276,000	$275,000	$279,000
4.50%	$247,000	$322,000	$266,000	$349,000	$289,000	$364,000
5.50%	$257,000	$395,000	$278,000	$442,000	$303,000	$474,000
6.50%	$267,000	$484,000	$291,000	$558,000	$319,000	$616,000

Chapter 5

The Greatest Risk to your Retirement Plan

I believe the greatest threat to achieving and maintaining the retirement lifestyle you want is that of your investments performing poorly for an extended period just before or in the early years of your retirement. This threat is known as the "sequence of returns" risk. This risk may significantly reduce the income available during retirement. The potential impact is that you either outlive your savings or are forced to significantly reduce your spending, especially in your latter years when you may need it the most. Think 2008 when the market lost almost half its value, and although it recovered over the next 10 years, it was devastating to those that retired then.

Two retirees starting with the exact same investment amounts can have entirely different financial results, depending on how the economy is performing near the start of their retirement, even if the long-term market averages are the same. For example, a person entering retirement near the beginning of a bear market will see a reduction in the overall return of that portfolio because of how much had to be withdrawn early in retirement when values were down. Also, this retiree must withdraw funds as his or her investments are losing value. Consequently, with less equities in the portfolio this retiree will not be able to benefit as much when the market recovers.

By contrast, someone who retires near the beginning of a bull market when stock prices are rising, lets this investor take early withdrawals of higher value investments, because they are rising in value and most likely will have a higher overall investment return than the bear market retiree earns. The reason is the bull market retiree has more equities remaining in the portfolio which can allow this retiree to benefit from continued strong market returns later in retirement.

What many retirees do not consider is the sequence in which these returns occur. Even though the market has returned 7 to 9% per year on average and may continue to average this over the next 30 years, there is no way you will know which years and for how many years the market will be up and which years it will be down. Therefore, I believe one of the biggest risks to your retirement is not the risk that the markets will go down significantly as they will do from time to time. The real risk is that the very worst returns occur in the early years of your retirement.

However, Investors have some options to better protect their investments against this risk, including the following:

- Having a cash cushion that can cover several years of expenses will lessen the need to significantly reduce spending or reduce the need to sell more risky investments when the values are down. Many financial advisors recommend having two to three years' worth of cash to be able to reduce the sequence of returns risk.

- Delay retirement and the need to make withdrawals until the market's performance improves. Not only will this allow you to leave your investments untapped for a longer period, but it will give you a chance to increase your savings. It might also allow you to delay Social Security and raise your benefits. Continuing to make contributions to retirement funds will allow you to buy at lower prices during the market downturn and provide for investments to continue to grow.

- A part-time job is a good way to supplement your income to reduce the need for larger savings withdrawals and buy time for your investments to grow, providing more options later in life. It is also an inexpensive way to occupy your newfound free time.

- Use a withdrawal system based on a percentage of the previous year's investment balance such as the 1/N, RMD, or VPW withdrawal system. This may be painful, requiring significant reductions in spending by delaying all discretionary expenses and implementing cost cutting measures until your investments recover.

- **33** -

On a personal note, in 2006 I decided I would like to retire at the end of 2010 at the age of 66. I was fortunate to have a job I liked, and when the great recession hit in 2008 and my portfolio fell close to 30%, I decided to delay my retirement plans and continue to work to prevent having to sell and withdraw any investments, thus giving more time for my investments to grow and recover. I was also able to continue to invest in my 401K and Roth IRA.

Rebalancing my portfolio at the beginning of each year, allowed me to replenish my stock ratio which had fallen to where it required me to buy more stock to increase the ratio to the target ratio, which at that time, was close to 60%. As stock prices steadily rose, my portfolio had more than recovered the entire drop in value by 2012. This allowed me to ease into retirement by reducing my workload gradually, until the end of 2015 when I fully retired.

Chapter *6*

Set Spending Limits

If you chose to use the 4% withdrawal system as your withdrawal method you can skip this chapter and go to Chapter 7, since this approach does not allow your withdrawal amounts to vary each year except to accommodate for inflation, and therefore is not based on how your investments are performing. With the other withdrawal systems, the amount you can withdraw each year will depend on the value of your investments at the end of the previous year. In order to reduce the potential for significant changes in spending from year to year, this chapter explains the benefits of using one of three spending limit systems.

The best system to use is to not set any limits and just adjust your spending up or down depending on the performance of your investments the previous year. This provides the greatest chance that you will not have to make significant cuts to your spending in the later years of your retirement even if a series of poor performing investment years occur over an extended period. This approach requires a lot of discretionary spending flexibility and the ability to reduce spending significantly in poor performing years. Many of us do not have this amount of spending flexibility, especially if we experience several years in a row of a poor performing portfolio.

As previously stated, a 20% drop in your portfolio value could result in a 20% or more drop in the suggested withdrawal amount from the previous year. Since 1970 the S&P 500 index of stocks has fallen 20% or more only 3 times with the worst years having dropped 38.5% in 2008, 29.7% in 1974, 23.4% in 2002, 17.4% in 1973, and 13.0% in 2001. Remember that future market performance may be better or worse than historical performances. (See Appendix II Table 5A for historical financial performance data).

Setting Lower & Upper Spending Limit Percentages:

If like many people your discretionary spending is limited, then setting a lower spending limit percent based on the amount you can afford to reduce spending will help reduce the impact of down years. Keep in mind that the lower the lower limit percent amount is that you set, you must also lower the upper limit percent so that in up years you do not spend all the extra that may be available, leaving some of it to help offset the down years.

This spending limit approach was based on a study by Vanguard describing the benefits of setting a ceiling and floor amount to spending. I changed the definition of ceiling to setting a **Lower Limit,** that suggests spending will not drop below this limit, and changed the definition of floor to setting an **Upper Limit**, that suggests spending will not go above this limit.

Worksheets 5, 6, or 7 are where you can set the Upper & Lower limit percentages. If your spending is flexible enough, I would suggest setting the lower limit to as high as 15% to ensure greater success if it becomes necessary to reduce spending. If you used Worksheet 1 to establish your spending budget and you calculated the Budget Flexibility % at the bottom of the Worksheet, I would suggest using a similar percentage for the lower limit or a percentage reduction you are comfortable with.

It is important to set the upper limit percentage amount to be equal to or lower than the lower limit so that in a good year you limit how much extra you can spend to help balance the portfolio up years with the down years. Keep in mind that setting lower and upper spending limits does not prevent having to reduce spending more than the lower limit suggests if a substantial decline in your portfolio occurs over several periods during retirement.

Creating a separate reserve fund:

Although this is the system I use, I do not recommend this method unless you are very comfortable with how it works, are willing to keep a record of the balance amount and have some spending flexibility. The reason I created it, and began using it in 2014, was to provide more control and flexibility over how you spend your money from one year to the next compared to the fixed spending limits. If the reserve fund is positive and you want to spend more that year than the withdrawal system determines, you can use it to pay for a special or unplanned expense.

It is a separate fund and cannot be considered as part of your portfolio value that is used to calculate the suggested withdrawal amount. The fund amount will reduce your withdrawal amount slightly by the percentage of the fund amount divided by the total available portfolio amount. You decide on the reserve fund starting amount. I would suggest starting the reserve fund with an amount equal to 25% of the previous year's spending amount.

Using the example of a 65-year-old retiree with a $500,000 portfolio, a 5% withdrawal rate, and having spent $55,000 the previous year, he would start the reserve fund at $13,750 (25% x $55,000). He would then subtract the reserve fund amount from the previous year-ending available portfolio amount prior to calculating the current year withdrawal amount. In this example, the withdrawal amount only drops $687 from $25,000 to $24,313 or 2.8%.

This reserve fund can be an actual separate account with actual money in it, or it can be a hypothetical reserve fund. Mine is hypothetical which required setting up a record keeping system to track the amount each year. In either case, you would add to or reduce the fund depending on the difference between the *desired* spending amount and the calculated *suggested* amount based on the withdrawal system you selected.

If the previous year portfolio performance was poor, and the suggested withdrawal amount is less than your desired amount, you must decide how much to reduce the reserve fund and use it to make up for some of the spending shortfall and how much to reduce spending. If the suggested withdrawal amount is greater than your desired amount, decide how much of the difference you want to add to spending and how much to save and put into the reserve fund to save for future down years. Worksheet 3 "Total Spendable Value of Your Portfolio" includes an entry for this optional reserve fund.

Keep in mind that if the reserve fund gets depleted due to several poor performing years you will have to decide to either re-fund it, reduce spending, or switch to using upper and lower spending limits.

Chapter 7

Bring it All Together

This chapter is the heart of the workbook and will answer the two questions raised at the beginning; *How much can I safely spend in retirement each year* and *If I need or want to spend more than my expected income, how much of my savings can I safely withdraw each year so that I do not outlive my savings.*

If you have not requested and received the companion computerized spreadsheet program, now would be a good time to do so. With the program you can fill out the worksheets faster and/or do What-If analysis and comparisons easily.

Worksheet 1: Establish your desired Spending

The Worksheet on page 41 is where you will create your *Desired* spending budget. Your spending budget should be created at the beginning of each year. If you kept track of the previous year's spending it will be a big help in creating the current year budget. If you already have a spending budget system that you prefer to use, you can simply enter the total annual estimated spending amount in the appropriate Withdrawals Worksheet 4, 5, 6, or 7 that you have decided to use.

It is very desirable to separate your budget into Essential *Needs* and Discretionary *Wants* to determine the amount of flexibility your spending plan will have in order to adjust for possible investment down years. Using

- 39 -

Worksheet 1, you can calculate the percent flexibility your budget has by dividing the Total discretionary expenses by the Total of all expenses.

The goal is to create as realistic a spending budget as possible. Keeping track and recording what was spent each month helps you see where your money goes and how realistic your budget is. It also helps you see where you might be able to adjust your spending and helps improve accuracy over time. See Appendix III How Am I Doing? for a form to use to track annual expenses, Income, and Portfolio value over time.

Keep in mind that you are creating a "Desired" spending budget, and it may have to be adjusted based on what the withdrawal system you selected "Suggests" you can spend. It first determines the "Safe" savings withdrawal amount and adds your expected after-tax income to arrive at the "Suggested" spending budget.

Note that if you choose the 4% Withdrawal System, you only need to fill this worksheet at the beginning of your retirement and not annually, but I recommend doing it at the beginning of every year so you can track how your spending plan is doing over time.

If you use the worksheet to create your spending budget, the "Monthly $" column is only used as a reference for those expenses that are close to the same every month but must then be annualized and entered into the "Annual $" column.

Worksheet 1: Establishing your Desired Spending

Create at the beginning of each Year				

Essential expenses:	ESTIMATED EXPENSES		ACTUAL EXPENSES	
	Monthly $	Annual $	Annual $	Over Budget
Housing:				
Mortgage or Rent				
Property taxes				
Homeowners insurance				
Utilities Water Gas Electric				
TV Phone & Internet				
Association Fees				
Maintenance/fees				
Other				
Food & Transportation:				
Groceries				
Auto Loan or lease payments				
Vehicle maintenance				
Fuel				
Auto insurance & Registration				
Public transportation				
Other				
Health care:				
Medical, Dental & Vision				
Medications and supplies				
Medicare/Medigap insurance				
Health insurance				
Other				
Personal insurance:				
Life insurance				
Disability insurance				
Long-term care insurance				
Other insurance				
Personal & Family care:				
Products and services				
Alimony Payment				
Child or Parent care				
Other				

Worksheet 1 Continued

Miscellaneous:	ESTIMATED EXPENSES		ACTUAL EXPENSES	
	Monthly $	Annual $	Annual $	Over Budget
Loans				
Pet Costs				
Banking & credit card fees				
Financial & Tax prep fees				
Other				
Total Essential expenses:				

Discretionary expenses:				
Entertainment				
Clothing				
Dinning out				
Travel/vacation				
Hobbies				
Subscriptions				
Memberships				
Gifts				
Charitable contributions				
Education				
Other Discretionary				
Total Discretionary expenses:				

Total All expenses:				

Budget Flexibility %:	
Divide Total Discretionary by Total all expenses	

Note the "Monthly $" column is only used as a reference for those expenses that are close to the same every month but must also be annualized and entered into the "Annual $" column.

Worksheet 2: Expected Annual After-Tax Income

This Worksheet is where you will identify your sources of retirement income. Enter your estimated income for the current year, and at the beginning of each year in retirement. You will also need to estimate income taxes to determine your estimated after-tax spendable income. After you stop working you will be responsible for withholding taxes on income from taxable accounts and other sources of income including withdrawals from 401K or IRA accounts and capital gains that you did not have income tax withheld. You may also have to pay income tax on your Social Security income depending on how much other income you receive.

You may be required to make quarterly tax payments, so it is a good idea to carefully review possible future tax implications that will reduce your spendable income. You may need to consult with a Tax professional and or Financial Planner if you are not comfortable with these determinations.

Note that if you choose the 4% Withdrawal System, you only need to fill this worksheet at the beginning of your retirement and not annually, but I recommend doing it at the beginning of every year so you can track how your plan is doing over time.

- 43 -

Worksheet 2: Expected Annual After-Tax Income

	Create at the beginning of each Year		

	Current Year Income		
	You	**Your Partner**	
Social Security:			
Pensions:			
Annuities:			
Employment Income:			
Rental Income:			
Dividend & Interest #1:			(Note 1 below)
Dividend & Interest #2:			
Other Income #1:			
Other Income #2:			
Other Income #3:			
Total Annual Income:			
Less Federal Income Tax:			(Note 2 below)
Less State Income Tax:			
Less Other Taxes:			
Total Annual After Tax Income:			(See Note 3 below)

Notes:

(1) Do not include any Dividends that are reinvested in stocks or bonds

(2) It should be noted that any income taxes that you may owe due to withdrawing from your investments including IRA RMD's should be estimated and entered into this section. Enter as Negative Numbers

(3) Combine amounts & enter total in the appropriate Withdrawal Worksheet. If you have your own estimated annual income system just enter the amount in the Withdrawal Worksheet instead of using this expected income sheet. Make sure the amount is the Annual After-Tax Income.

- 44 -

Worksheet 3: Total Spendable Value of Your Portfolio

Use this worksheet to estimate the total savings & investments available to be withdrawn from, over the length of your retirement, to support your desired lifestyle. It should not include the value of Annuities, Life Insurance, Home, Auto or other personal items of value that may be difficult to convert to spendable money.

It will allow you to allocate money for an Emergency Fund, any money you want to leave to your heirs or be used as a cushion for the later years of retirement and include a reserve fund as discussed in Chapter 6. These amounts are subtracted from the total to determine the Spendable portion of your Savings & Investments. This amount is used in the appropriate Withdrawals Worksheet to arrive at the suggested safe withdrawal amount. Note that the amounts entered in this worksheet should be the previous year ending amount.

If you choose the RMD withdrawal system, it will most likely leave money in your portfolio at the end, due to its conservative nature as explained in Chapters 3 and 4. If you allocated money to be used as a cushion or hedge that you live longer than planned, you might consider reducing or eliminating the amount, because this amount is subtracted each year from your portfolio amount before the withdrawal amount is calculated. This reduces your annual withdrawal amount that you could have spent.

Unexpected major expenses happen, so money should be set aside for these unplanned non budgeted expenses. If your income sources are mostly guaranteed, then the emergency fund only needs to cover the expense and not lost wages so it can be much lower than during your working years.

Note that if you choose the 4% Withdrawal System you only need to fill this worksheet at the beginning of your retirement and not annually, but I recommend doing it at the beginning of every year so you can track how your plan is doing over time.

Worksheet 3: Total Spendable Value of Your Portfolio

Total Portfolio amount available to be spent during retirement **Create at the beginning of each Year**		

	Value End of Previous Year	See Notes below
Savings #1:		
Savings #2:		If you have more savings & Investment Accounts Than Listed combine accounts
Savings #3:		
Investment #1:		
Investment #2:		
Investment #3:		
Investment #4:		
Investment #5:		
Investment #6:		
Roth IRA #1		
Roth IRA #2		
IRA or 401K #1:		
IRA or 401K #2:		
IRA or 401K #3:		
Savings & Investment Total:		
Credit Card Balances:		
Emergency Fund:		
Bequeaths to Heirs:		
Cushion if you live longer than planned		
Optional Reserve Fund:		
Total Reductions:		

Total Portfolio amount available to spend in retirement:		**Subtract Total reductions from Savings & Investment total**

Notes:

(1) Do not include the value of Annuities, Life Insurance, Home, Auto
    or other personal items.

(2) Enter the Total Portfolio amount available to be spent in retirement
    in the appropriate Withdrawal System Worksheet that is selected.

Worksheets 4, 5, 6, or 7

After selecting the retirement withdrawal system that you are most comfortable, complete the appropriate Worksheet, either 4, 5, 6 or 7. This is probably the hardest and most important decision you will need to make in order to create a successful retirement spending and withdrawal plan. You may want to reread chapters 3 & 4 or seek additional professional help so that you are comfortable with the system you choose.

You may want to compare withdrawal systems by filling out more than one worksheet to see how they compare. If you have not requested and received the companion computerized spreadsheet program, now would be a good time to do so. With the program you can fill out the worksheets faster and/or do What-If analysis and comparisons easily.

To begin, enter your current age, the age you want your savings to last to, your desired annual spending amount, your annual after-tax income, and the total investment amounts that were all determined in Worksheets 1,2 and 3. The selected worksheet will then determine how much if any shortfall there is that needs to be withdrawn from your savings and see if your desired spending plan is realistic compared to what the worksheet suggests you can spend. If the shortfall is less than the suggested withdrawal amount based on the withdrawal system you choose, your plan is good and may even allow you to increase your spending. Conversely, if the shortfall is greater than the suggested withdrawal amount, you may have to reduce your spending based on the limits you set.

NOTE if you choose Worksheet 4 with the 4% Withdrawal System, you will only fill out the worksheet once at the beginning of your retirement. The other three withdrawal systems require recalculating your withdrawal amount at the beginning of each year based on the value of your available investments ending the previous December 31st.

It is very important that you do not attempt to change withdrawal systems or change expected investment gains or other variables used from year to year without a thorough understanding of the implications those changes may have on the success of your retirement.

CAUTION: As stated previously, the future may contain scenarios that are better or worse than anything considered by this workbook. It is also important to remember that, despite the sophistication of the methods used, this workbook makes several simplifying assumptions. Note that the Suggested Withdrawal amounts are just that, Suggestions, and are designed to prevent you from significantly over or under spending your savings. It is highly recommended that you seek additional guidance in developing a retirement plan with which you will be most comfortable.

Worksheet 4: Instructions for Using the 4% Withdrawal System

Line No. 1: Enter Current Year

Line No. 2: Enter Current Age at start of current year

Line No. 3: Enter Age at which your savings should be depleted

Line No. 4: Subtract Line 2 from Line 3 to get years remaining for your savings to last

Line No. 5: Enter "Total All Expenses" from Worksheet 1

Line No. 6: Enter "Total Annual After-Tax Income" from Worksheet 2

Line No. 7: Enter "Total Portfolio amount available to spend in retirement" from Worksheet 3

Line No. 8: Subtract Line 6 from Line 5 to get Desired Withdrawal Amount

Line No. 9: Enter number found in the "Divisor" column of Table 2 based on years left as shown in line 4.

Line No. 10: Divide Line 7 by Line 9 to get Suggested First Year Withdrawals

Line No. 11: Subtract Line 8 from Line 10. This will be the amount that can be added to your desired spending budget if it is a positive number or subtracted from your desired spending budget if it is a negative number.

Line No. 12: Add Lines 6, 8, & 11 to arrive at the amount you can safely spend in the first year of your retirement.

Remember this Worksheet is only used once at the start of your retirement. The amount on line 10 which is the Suggested first year withdrawal amount will then be increased for inflation each year thereafter.

Worksheet 4: Using the 4% Withdrawal System

Use this Worksheet only At The Beginning of your first year of retirement
See Note at bottom of this Worksheet

Line No.		
1		Current Year
2		Current Age at Start of the year
3		Age Savings should End or be depleted
4		Years you want your Savings to last
5		Desired Total Spending for Year
6		Estimated Total Annual After Tax Income
7		Total Spendable Value of your Portfolio at start of retirement
8		Desired Withdrawal Amount
9		Suggested "Divisor" number from Table 2
10		Suggested First Year Withdrawal
11		Amount above or below the Desired Withdrawal amount
12		Suggested Amount You Could Safely Spend in The First Year Of Your Retirement

Note: In subsequent years increase Line 10 amount by the previous year's
inflation rate and add it to your expected income for the year
to arrive at the new safe spending amount.

- 50 -

Table 2:   4% Withdrawal System

Years Left	Divisor	Equivalent %	Years Left	Divisor	Equivalent %
38	29.45	3.40%	19	16.73	5.98%
37	28.86	3.46%	18	15.96	6.27%
36	28.27	3.54%	17	15.18	6.59%
35	27.66	3.61%	16	14.38	6.95%
34	27.05	3.70%	15	13.58	7.36%
33	26.43	3.78%	14	12.76	7.84%
32	25.80	3.88%	13	11.93	8.38%
31	25.16	3.97%	12	11.09	9.01%
30	24.51	4.08%	11	10.24	9.77%
29	23.86	4.19%	10	9.37	10.67%
28	23.19	4.31%	9	8.50	11.77%
27	22.51	4.44%	8	7.61	13.15%
26	21.83	4.58%	7	6.70	14.92%
25	21.13	4.73%	6	5.79	17.29%
24	20.42	4.90%	5	4.85	20.60%
23	19.71	5.07%	4	3.91	25.57%
22	18.98	5.27%	3	2.95	33.86%
21	18.24	5.48%	2	1.98	50.46%
20	17.49	5.72%	1	1.00	100.00%

Worksheet 5: Instructions for using the 1/N Withdrawal System

Line No. 1: Enter Current Year

Line No. 2: Enter Current Age at start of current year

Line No. 3: Enter Age at which your savings should be depleted

Line No. 4: Subtract Line 2 from Line 3 to get years remaining for your savings to last

Line No. 5: Enter "Total All Expenses" from Worksheet 1

Line No. 6: Enter "Total Annual After-Tax Income" from Worksheet 2

Line No. 7: Enter "Total Portfolio amount available to spend in retirement" from Worksheet 3

Line No. 8: Subtract Line 6 from Line 5 to get Desired Withdrawal Amount

Line No. 9: Divide Line 7 by Line 4 to get the Suggested Annual Withdrawal

Line No. 10: Subtract Line 8 from Line 9. This will be the amount that can be added to your desired spending budget if it is a positive number or subtracted from your desired spending budget if it is a negative number.

Line No. 11: Skip if no spending limits are needed or a reserve fund is used, otherwise set the spending limit to a percentage that you are comfortable with. The higher the better. If you are comfortable using the Budget Flexibility % calculated at the bottom of worksheet 1 use this percentage. **Enter the percentage as a negative number.** See Chapter 6 on setting limits if needed.

Line No. 12: If a percentage is entered on line 11 multiply it by line 5. Should be a negative number.

Line No. 13: Skip if no spending limits are needed or a reserve fund is used, otherwise set it to a percentage equal to that on line 11 but no more than 15%. **Enter the percentage as a positive number**. See Chapter 6 on setting limits if needed.

Line No. 14: If a percentage is entered on line 13 multiply it by line 5. Should be a positive number.

Line No. 15: If you set Lower and Upper Spending limits and line 10 is negative, then enter the lessor amount between line 10 and line 12. Conversely if line 10 is a positive number, enter the lessor amount between line 10 and line 14.

If no spending limit is needed, then enter the amount from line 10. If line 10 is negative enter the amount as a negative number.

If a reserve fund is used, then decide how much of line 10 will be entered as an adjustment to spending. If line 10 is negative decide how much of this amount you want to reduce by using some of your reserve fund if any and enter the reduced amount as a negative amount on line 15. You will then need to reduce your reserve account by the amount you reduced line 10.

Conversely if the amount on line 10 is positive again decide how much if any of this amount you want to use to increase spending and enter this amount as a positive number on line 15. You will then need to add the amount you elected not to spend of line 10, to your reserve account.

Line No. 16: Add Line 5 and line 15 to arrive at the suggested amount you can Safely spend for the year.

Worksheet 5: Using the 1/N Withdrawal System

	Create at the beginning of each Year	

Line No.		
1		Current Year
2		Current Age at Start of the year
3		Age Savings should End or be depleted
4		Years remaining for your Savings to last
5		Desired Total Spending for Year
6		Estimated Total Annual After Tax Income
7		Total Spendable Value of your Portfolio at the beginning of the year
8		Desired Withdrawal Amount
9		Suggested Annual Withdrawal
10		Amount above or below the Desired Withdrawal amount
11		Lower Spending Limit % (See Note below)
12		
13		Upper Spending Limit % (See Note below)
14		
15		Spending Limit Adjustment
16		Suggested Amount You Could Safely Spend for the year

NOTE: If no limits are needed or a reserve fund is used skip lines 11 thru 14
If Lower & Upper spending limit % is used choose these
limits carefully. The limit % used should not be changed in future
years if possible since you run the risk of over spending and having to
make significant spending reductions In the later years of retirement.
See Chapter 6 for more details.

Worksheet 6: Instructions for using the RMD Withdrawal System

Line No. 1: Enter Current Year

Line No. 2: Enter Current Age at start of current year. Must be 62 or higher.

Line No. 3: Enter "Total All Expenses" from Worksheet 1

Line No. 4: Enter "Total Annual After-Tax Income" from Worksheet 2

Line No. 5: Enter "Total Portfolio amount available to spend in retirement" from Worksheet 3

Line No. 6: Subtract Line 4 from Line 3 to get Desired Withdrawal Amount

Line No. 7: Enter the "Divisor" number found in Table 3 based on your current age as shown in line 2.

Line No. 8: Divide Line 5 by Line 7 to get the Suggested Annual Withdrawal amount.

Line No. 9: Subtract Line 6 from Line 8. This will be the amount that can be added to your desired spending budget if it is a positive number or subtracted from your desired spending budget if it is a negative number.

Line No. 10: Skip if no spending limits are needed or a reserve fund is used, otherwise set the spending limit to a percentage that you are comfortable with. The higher the better. If you are comfortable using the Budget Flexibility % calculated at the bottom of worksheet 1 use this percentage. **Enter the percentage as a negative number.** See Chapter 6 on setting limits if needed.

Line No. 11: If a percentage is entered on line 10 multiply it by line 3. Should be a negative number.

Line No. 12: Skip if no spending limits are needed or a reserve fund is used, otherwise set it to a percentage equal to that on line 10 but no more than 15%. **Enter the percentage as a positive number**. See Chapter 6 on setting limits if needed.

Line No. 13: If a percentage is entered on line 12 multiply it by line 3. Should be a positive number.

Line No. 14: If you set Lower and Upper Spending limits and line 9 is negative, then enter the lessor amount between line 9 and line 11. Conversely if line 9 is a positive number, enter the lessor amount between line 9 and line 13.

If no spending limit is needed, then enter the amount from line 9. If line 9 is negative enter the amount as a negative number.

If a reserve fund is used, then decide how much of line 9 will be entered as an adjustment to spending. If line 9 is negative decide how much of this amount you want to reduce by using some of your reserve fund if any and enter the reduced amount as a negative amount on line 14. You will then need to reduce your reserve account by the amount you reduced line 9.

Conversely if the amount on line 9 is positive again decide how much if any of this amount you want to use to increase spending and enter this amount as a positive number on line 14. You will then need to add the amount you elected not to spend of line 9, to your reserve account.

Line No. 15: Add Lines 3 and line14 to arrive at the suggested amount you can Safely spend for the year.

Worksheet 6: Using the RMD Withdrawal System

Create at the beginning of each Year		

Line No.		
1		Current Year
2		Current Age. Must be 62 or higher
3		Desired Total Spending for Year
4		Estimated Total Annual After Tax Income
5		Total Spendable Value of your Portfolio at the beginning of the year
6		Desired Withdrawal Amount
7		Suggested Withdrawal Divisor Table 3
8		Suggested Annual Withdrawal
9		Amount above or below the Desired Withdrawal amount
10		Lower Spending Limit % (See Note below)
11		
12		Upper Spending Limit % (See Note below)
13		
14		Spending Limit Adjustment
15		Suggested Amount You Could Safely Spend for the year

If Lower & Upper spending limit % is used choose these limits carefully. The limit % used should not be changed in future years if possible since you run the risk of over spending and having to make significant spending reductions In the later years of retirement. See Chapter 6 for more details if needed.

Table 3: RMD Withdrawal System

Your Age at the beginning of the current year	Withdrawal Divisor	Your Age at the beginning of the current year	Withdrawal Divisor
62	33.8	82	16.3
63	32.9	83	15.5
64	32.0	84	14.8
65	31.1	85	14.1
66	30.2	86	13.4
67	29.2	87	12.7
68	28.3	88	12.0
69	27.4	89	11.4
70	26.5	90	10.8
71	25.6	91	10.2
72	24.7	92	9.6
73	23.8	93	9.1
74	22.9	94	8.6
75	22.0	95	8.1
76	21.2	96	7.6
77	20.3	97	7.1
78	19.5	98	6.7
79	18.7	99	6.3
80	17.9	100	5.9
81	17.1		

Worksheet 7: Instructions for using the VPW Withdrawal System

Line No. 1: Enter Current Year

Line No. 2: Enter Current Age at start of current year

Line No. 3: Enter Age at which your savings should be depleted

Line No. 4: Subtract Line 2 from Line 3 to get years remaining for your savings to last

Line No. 5: Enter "Total All Expenses" from Worksheet 1

Line No. 6: Enter "Total Annual After-Tax Income" from Worksheet 2

Line No. 7: Enter "Total Portfolio amount available to spend in retirement" from Worksheet 3

Line No. 8: Subtract Line 6 from Line 5 to get Desired Withdrawal Amount

Line No. 9: Enter the "Divisor" number found in Table 4 based on years left as shown in line 4 and your closest stock to bond ratio at the beginning of the year.

Line No. 10: Divide Line 7 by Line 9 to get the Suggested Annual Withdrawal amount.

Line No. 11: Subtract Line 8 from Line 10. This is the amount above (positive number) or below (negative number) the desired withdrawal amount.

Line No. 12: Skip if no spending limits are needed or a reserve fund is used otherwise, set the spending limit to a percentage that you are comfortable with. The higher the better. If you are comfortable using the Budget Flexibility % calculated at the bottom of worksheet 1 use this percentage. **Enter the percentage as a negative number.** See Chapter 6 on setting limits if needed.

Line No. 13: If a percentage is entered on line 12 multiply it by line 5. Should be a negative number.

Line No. 14: Skip if no spending limits are needed or a reserve fund is used otherwise set it to a percentage equal to that on line 12 but no more than 15%. **Enter the percentage as a positive number**. See Chapter 6 on setting limits if needed.

Line No. 15: If a percentage is entered on line 14 multiply it by line 5. Should be a positive number.

Line No. 16: If you set Lower and Upper Spending limits and line 11 is negative then enter the lessor amount between line 11 and line 13. Conversely if line 11 is a positive number enter the lessor amount between line 11 and line 15.

If no spending limit is needed, then enter the amount on line 11. If line 11 is negative enter the amount as a negative number.

If a reserve fund is used, then decide how much of line 11 will be entered as an adjustment to spending. If line 11 is negative decide how much of this amount you want to reduce by using some of your reserve fund if any and enter the reduced amount as a negative amount on line 16. You will then need to reduce your reserve account by the amount you reduced line 11.

Conversely if the amount on line 11 is positive again decide how much if any of this amount you want to use to increase spending and enter this amount as a positive number on line 16. You will then need to add the amount you elected not to spend of line 11, to your reserve account.

Line No. 17: Add Line 5 and line 16 to arrive at the suggested amount you can Safely spend for the year.

Worksheet 7: Using the VPW Withdrawal System

	Create at the beginning of each Year	

Line No.		
1		Current Year
2		Current Age at Start of the year
3		Age Savings should End or be depleted
4		Years remaining for your Savings to last
5		Desired Total Spending for Year
6		Estimated Total Annual After Tax Income
7		Total Spendable Value of your Portfolio at the beginning of the year
8		Desired Withdrawal Amount
9		Suggested Withdrawal Divisor Table 4
10		Suggested Annual Withdrawal
11		Amount above or below the Desired Withdrawal amount
12		Lower Spending Limit % (See Note below)
13		
14		Upper Spending Limit % (See Note below)
15		
16		Spending Limit Adjustment
17		Suggested Amount You Could Safely Spend for the year

NOTE: If no limits are needed or a reserve fund is used skip lines 12 thru 15
If Lower & Upper spending limit % is used choose these limits carefully. The limit % used should not be changed in future years if possible since you run the risk of over spending and having to make significant spending reductions In the later years of retirement.
See Chapter 6 for more details if needed.

Table 4: VPW Withdrawal System Divisors

Years Left	VPW Stock to Bond ratio			
	20/80	40/60	60/40	80/20
38	25.00	22.73	20.83	19.23
37	25.00	22.73	20.41	18.87
36	24.39	22.22	20.41	18.87
35	23.81	21.74	20.00	18.52
34	23.26	21.28	19.61	18.18
33	22.73	21.28	19.23	17.86
32	22.22	20.83	18.87	17.86
31	21.74	20.41	18.52	17.54
30	21.28	20.00	18.18	17.24
29	20.83	19.61	17.86	16.95
28	20.41	19.23	17.54	16.67
27	20.00	18.52	17.24	16.39
26	19.61	18.18	16.95	15.87
25	18.87	17.86	16.39	15.63
24	18.18	17.24	16.13	15.38
23	17.86	16.67	15.63	14.93
22	17.24	16.39	15.15	14.49
21	16.67	15.63	14.71	14.08
20	15.87	15.15	14.29	13.70
19	15.38	14.71	13.89	13.33
18	14.71	14.08	13.33	12.82
17	14.08	13.51	12.82	12.35
16	13.33	12.82	12.20	11.76
15	12.66	12.20	11.63	11.24
14	12.05	11.63	11.11	10.75
13	11.24	10.87	10.42	10.20
12	10.53	10.20	9.80	9.62
11	9.71	9.52	9.17	8.93
10	9.01	8.77	8.47	8.33
9	8.20	8.00	7.75	7.63
8	7.35	7.19	7.04	6.90
7	6.49	6.41	6.25	6.17
6	5.65	5.56	5.46	5.41
5	4.76	4.72	4.65	4.59
4	3.86	3.82	3.79	3.76
3	2.92	2.91	2.89	2.87
2	1.98	1.97	1.96	1.96
1	1.00	1.00	1.00	1.00

The above table is based on a table Collaboratively developed by a group of Bogleheads®. www.bogleheads.org

Chapter *8*

Which Accounts to Withdraw from and in what order

After you determine how much to withdraw from your investments to support your retirement lifestyle in the new year, you will need to determine which accounts you should withdraw from and in what order. *When* you withdraw money from your investments is not nearly as important as deciding *What* investments need to be sold to fund your retirement. Studies have shown that what types of assets such as cash, stocks and bonds you withdraw from can have a big impact on how well your investments grow long term.

This program assumes the entire suggested annual withdrawal amount for the new year is determined and withdrawn at the beginning of the year to be conservative but when you withdraw it or how often is up to you. Withdrawing closer to when you need to spend it may allow your investment to grow longer.

In what order should you withdraw:

The order in which you withdraw funds can have a significant effect on income taxes, so the goal should be to try and minimize the impact of taxes while maximizing investment returns.

If you or your spouse have tax differed accounts like IRA's and 401K's (Not Roth IRA's) you may be required by the IRS to withdraw a minimum amount based on your age to avoid a 50% penalty being assessed by the IRS for not withdrawing enough. This is known as the RMD amount or **R**equired **M**inimum **D**istribution amount. The IRS allowed you to put the money into the account tax-free but once you reach a certain age, they want those tax dollars back! Always withdraw this amount first to determine if you need to withdraw more from your savings to meet your spending needs. The rules regarding the age you must start taking the RMD changed with the passing of the SECURE Act which became law on December 20, 2019. You should consult IRS publication 590-B Distributions from IRA's and a tax specialist if uncomfortable with this topic.

You do not have to spend the RMD amount so long as you pay the income tax due. If it is more than you need, you can invest it in a taxable account. It is important to note that if you only withdraw the minimum RMD required in the early years, it may push you into a higher income tax bracket in your later years. Withdrawing more money from accounts subject to RMDs during the early years of your retirement helps reduce the amount of your RMDs when you reach the required age to take the RMD, thus lowering the tax in your later years but possibly raise the amount of taxes you'll pay early in retirement. This may or may not be advantageous, so the key is to understand the rules and plan accordingly, to minimize your taxes and maximize your savings.

If additional withdrawals beyond the RMD amount are necessary to meet your spending needs, there are several methods, but each have varying tax consequences. One method is to withdraw a proportional amount between your taxable and tax deferred accounts. A proportional amount is withdrawn from each of your accounts based on the proportion of your retirement savings in each account type. This helps stretch your savings by spreading out the tax advantages that your retirement accounts offer, reducing significant swings in the amount of taxes you pay each year. Using this method should allow you to pay a similar amount in taxes each year. This also makes budgeting for taxes easier.

As an example, let's say you have $500,000 in total investments to draw from of which $100,000 is in taxable savings and brokerage accounts, $325,000 in a 401K and IRA and $75,000 in a Roth IRA. You have determined that you are required to withdraw $13,000 to meet the RMD requirement. Further you determined you need to withdraw $26,000 for the current year from your investments to fund your retirement after accounting for other sources of income. The proportional method would suggest withdrawing $5200 from

- 64 -

taxable savings ($100,000 divided by $500,000 equals 20% times $26,000 equals $5200). This leaves $20,800 to be withdrawn from your 401k and IRA which more than meets the RMD requirement.

Notice I am not suggesting you touch the Roth IRA because I believe it should contain your most aggressive investments that can grow tax free over the long term. However, you could tap the Roth for $3900 ($75,000 divided by $500,000 equals 15% times $26,000 equals $3900). This would reduce the amount needed from your 401K and IRA to $16,900 still meeting the RMD and would reduce your income tax for the current year, but it could force you to pay a higher tax in later years since you would have a slightly higher RMD to withdraw in the future.

Note that the RMD may force you to take out more from your traditional retirement accounts than the proportional amount suggests. Also keep in mind that the amount of your social security income subject to income taxes most likely will increase and therefore raise your total tax, so keeping your withdrawals from accounts subject to RMD's close to the minimum may make sense.

What type of assets to Sell?

Historical data suggests that your portfolio value can vary significantly even with the same portfolio and the same withdrawal rate, without changing your investments or taking on more risk. It depends on *what* asset classes such as cash, stocks and bonds you choose to sell. As Warren Buffet once said, "Be Fearful When Others Are Greedy and Greedy When Others Are Fearful". Buying assets when they are out of favor and selling them when they are in favor seems to make sense.

As an example, when you need to withdraw money from your portfolio, sell some of your most appreciated investments. So, in a Bear Market you would cash your money market and short-term bonds and hold longer term bonds

- 65 -

and stocks until a Bull Market returns and then sell longer term bonds and stocks when needed.

Conversely, it does not seem to make sense to live off your conservative cash and bond assets when stock markets are up. Yes, stocks could continue to go up, but they could easily go down since you cannot predict when the bull market ends or retracts. The challenge with this method is finding a reliable indicator, so you do not sell too early or too late in the market cycle. For more information regarding this and other interesting methods of maximizing your returns, See Appendix V Chapter 8 references.

Using this method also acts as a self-rebalancing mechanism, helping to keep your investments properly diversified. The reason is that as stocks rise in a bull market, your stock ratio increases above your target ratio so when it is time to rebalance you would need to reduce your stock holdings forcing you to sell high. Conversely, as stocks fall in a bear market the ratio falls below your target forcing you to buy stocks at depressed values. This is also true with bonds. The next chapter will explain the importance of portfolio rebalancing.

Chapter *9*

Thoughts on Investing for Diversification & Growth

After determining what investments accounts to sell and in what order, this chapter deals with the importance of where you should locate those accounts and how they should be allocated. It then deals with keeping those allocations in balance over time and introduces a method of diversification for safety and peace of mind.

Where to put your investments:

Where you put your investments or *asset location* can make a big difference in how much after-tax income you can earn over time. That's because different investments and different types of accounts are subject to different tax rules. Sorting your investments into accounts based on their tax efficiency or inefficiency has the potential to both lower your overall tax bill and defer paying taxes as long as possible.

You may want to consider putting the most tax-efficient investments in taxable accounts and the least tax-efficient in tax-deferred accounts like a traditional IRA, 401(k), or deferred annuity, or a tax-exempt account such as a Roth IRA or HSA. The more tax-inefficient an investment is, the more tax you pay on it every year if it's held in a taxable account.

Tax-inefficient funds generate interest payments that are taxed at ordinary income rates. Individual stocks if bought and held for at least a year are relatively tax-efficient because capital gains on the sale of stocks held for more than a year are currently taxed at a federal rate of 20%, 15% and in some cases, 0% depending on income.

In general, the most tax-efficient funds are most Index funds, tax-managed equity funds, and Municipal bond funds. Value index funds and small-cap index funds are moderately efficient. The most tax-inefficient funds consist of High-yield bond funds, high turnover active stock funds, and real estate funds (REITs). REITs are tax-inefficient because they are required by law to pay out at least 90% of their taxable income which is generally taxed at higher ordinary income rates. Equity-based exchange-traded funds (ETFs) are like stocks and in most cases are tax-efficient. Large-cap funds have historically tended to be more tax-efficient than similar small-cap funds.

In summary, I would recommend:

- Put tax efficient investments like stocks, Index funds, ETFs, I-Bonds, and Municipal Bonds in your taxable accounts. I further recommend putting high growth investments such as stocks and Index funds in a Roth IRA or Roth 401K where they can grow tax free for many years if you can avoid withdrawing them too early.

- Put tax inefficient investments such as Bonds, Bond funds as well as REITs in your tax deferred accounts like IRAs and 401Ks

For further information on this approach see Appendix V chapter 9 references.

The importance of Asset Allocation:

Several groundbreaking studies in the late 1980's and early 1990's including two by Gary P. Brinson, L. Rudolph Hood, and Gilbert L. Beebower, discovered that over 90% of the *variation* in a portfolio's return could be explained by how its funds were allocated among the three major asset classes of stocks, bonds, and cash, *and not by what funds were chosen to be in each asset class*. In other words, **asset allocation has a larger impact on overall portfolio results than the selection of specific securities**.

- 68 -

The findings of these studies have been widely misunderstood. It does not mean that 90% of the *annual rates of return* can be attributed to the allocation of assets, only 90% of the *variability* in returns. The goal of proper asset allocation is to reduce portfolio variability and thus risk.

Since each asset class have different potential average annual gains, along with different portfolio variability and their associated risks, these percentages or ratios should change based on your time horizon and how much risk you are willing to accept as you age. The key of course, is to determine what the percent of each asset class should be in your portfolio at any point in time. Cash is not normally considered an investment, so it should not be included when determining the amount of stocks and bonds to have in your portfolio.

There are lots of theories and approaches financial planners use and no one-size fits all. John Bogle, founder of Vanguard and author, advocates keeping it simple especially during retirement when you are needing to make withdrawals. For a relatively conservative low risk investor, he suggests a rough rule of thumb of subtracting your age from 100 to determine the percentage of stock, and your age in bonds. For a less conservative investor, subtracting from 110 would be more appropriate. Appendix II Table 5A, show various asset allocation ratios and their historical performances.

The Importance of Portfolio rebalancing:

Once you have chosen your asset mix of stocks, bonds, and cash, I am a strong believer in rebalancing your portfolio at the beginning of each year, or whenever significant withdrawals from the portfolio occur, in order to maintain your target allocation. The reason is that as stocks rise in a bull market, your stock ratio increases above your target ratio so when it is time to rebalance you would need to reduce your stock holdings, forcing you to sell high. Conversely, as stocks fall in a bear market the ratio falls below your target forcing you to buy stocks at low values. This is also true with bonds.

Following a disciplined rebalancing plan has the added benefit of removing the emotional decisions that occur when investors become brave in a bull market and do not want to miss out. Conversely, when stocks go down investors get scared and want to sell. Buying after large market gains means you are buying at more expensive prices and selling after big market losses means you are selling at cheaper prices. Buying high and selling low is not a very good investment strategy.

The Bucket Strategy:

The bucket strategy is a system that can provide extra insurance against several years of a down market which can really impact your investments, especially if it occurs early in retirement. Pioneered by Financial Planner Harold Evensky, the Bucket approach is simply a total-return portfolio combined with a cash component (Bucket 1) to meet near-term living expenses and avoid selling under-performing investments that are affected by market swings. The long-term portion of the portfolio is aimed towards maximizing the total return. Money taken from the long-term Bucket is periodically put into Bucket 1 to replenish it to meet living expenses.

Although there are many variations of the bucket approach, I prefer a three-bucket approach as follows:

Bucket 1: Years 1 thru 3

The goal of this portion of the portfolio is to put funds that have almost no risk of loss to fund near term living expenses. Producing income is secondary so it holds cash instruments and very short duration bonds or bond funds rather than higher yielding but riskier funds with the potential for losses.

This bucket provides both peace of mind and preventing investors from over-reacting to near term market swings thus removing some of the emotion in selling too soon. Investors should look to their expected portfolio withdrawals to determine how much cash should be held in this bucket. Holding three years of expected portfolio withdrawals to fund retirement in this bucket is a reasonable goal and three years provides some flexibility when you must sell investments in Bucket 2.

Bucket 2: Years 4 thru 10

Bucket 2 is designed to deliver a higher level of income than Bucket 1. Its goal is aimed at inflation protection with some amount of capital appreciation. The reason is that this portion of the portfolio has a longer time horizon, so inflation protection becomes a concern. Putting I-Bonds and other inflation protected securities that offer inflation protection without the volatility of more risky investments are recommended in this bucket. I would also recommend short term bond funds for money needing to be withdrawn in years 4 and 5, and intermediate bond funds or bond ladders for years 6 thru 10 as examples of investments that have low risk if held for their duration periods.

Of course, there are many other types of investments that can be held in this bucket, but the emphasis should be on lower risk with some inflation protection and the potential to recover loses within the bucket's time horizon based on historical returns.

Bucket 1 will eventually need to be replenished by Bucket 2, and the timing of filling Bucket 1 will depend on how your portfolio is performing. You would then sell the short duration bonds first.

Bucket 3: Years 11 and Beyond

The long-term portion of the portfolio contains more risky investments that provide for long-term growth, but also comes with more volatility, so you need a much longer period to recover from any reductions caused by extended bear markets. The theory is that historically since 1926 stocks have only lost

- 71 -

Copyrighted Material

value once if held for at least 10 years. While U.S. large-cap stocks lost money over that decade of 1999 to 2008, cash made money, Bonds made money, International stocks made money, Small caps made money. The key is to have a widely diversified portfolio and not have a high concentration in funds like the S&P 500 index fund that did not do well during this period.

When your portfolio of stocks has performed well, and especially when rebalancing your portfolio each year, you might consider selling your most appreciate stocks as discussed in chapter 8. There may be many years where Bucket 3 does not perform well. It will take discipline to realize it is okay to let Buckets 1 & 2 get to a lower level during these years. There will also be years when your portfolio performs well, and the buckets can be refilled.

As stated earlier, I believe the bucket approach provides both peace of mind and prevents investors from over-reacting to near term market swings, thus removing some of the emotion in selling too soon. For more information on the bucket method, see Appendix V Chapter 9 references.

Chapter *10*

Summary

I was planning to write a typical summary of key takeaways from each chapter but decided instead to share my retirement plan as an example of what we have learned and tried to incorporate into this workbook. My wife and I are near our mid 70's, and like all long-term plans, ours needed to be tweaked along the way. *Keep in mind that it may not be a plan that is best for your situation.*

First, we have chosen to have the portion of our savings that we want to spend in retirement, last through age 95. Second, we have chosen to use the VPW withdrawal system because we believe it provides us with the best balance between total withdrawals and withdrawal amounts in the early years of retirement versus the latter years. We are comfortable with this approach since we are reasonably healthy, with decent medical insurance, and want to spend more in the earlier years of retirement than the other systems allow and are okay with the lower amounts in the later years.

Our retirement plan is structured as follows:

- I delayed receiving social security benefits until age 70 and my wife until age 66. This resulted in a significant monthly benefit increase.

- Increased our spending flexibility by reducing the fixed portion of our spending by retiring to a lower tax state. We moved to a secure 55 + retirement community and bought a barrier free home with no stairs and two master bedroom suites so if one of us becomes disabled or needs in-home care we can both be comfortable and age in place as long as possible.

- Maintain a separate hypothetical reserve fund that sets spending limits to match spending flexibility (see Chapter 6).

- Calculate our RMD amount at the beginning of the year but withdraw it quarterly along with paying estimated taxes quarterly.

- When we need to withdraw money from our portfolio, we choose what to sell by selling the most appreciated assets, as outlined in Chapter 8.

- We withdraw the amounts proportionately among our taxable and tax deferred accounts to balance our taxes from year-to-year. We do not withdraw from our Roth tax free account, which contains stocks for long term growth.

- We use a three Bucket System for peace of mind and diversification as outlined in Chapter 9. This includes three years' worth of expected future withdrawals held in CD's and money market accounts.

- Maintain a 35/50/15 stock to bond to cash ratio since We are both near our mid 70's and comfortable with this level of risk. Notice I included the percentage of cash since as each year passes cash becomes a greater percentage of our portfolio. Without cash it would currently be about 40/60.

- Rebalance our portfolio at the beginning of the year, or when significant withdrawal amounts are taken. Try not to let the ratios fall outside a 10% band. So, for a 40% stock ratio adjust if below 36% or above 44%.

- We plan to purchase an inflation-indexed Single Premium Immediate Annuity or SPIA near our 80th birthday to hedge against one of us living past 95 which is the age we used to determine how long we want our portfolio to last. The SPIA is designed so that the monthly annuity payment plus all after tax income provides enough income to live comfortably and not be dependent on how well a shrinking portfolio performs. For more information on this approach see Appendix V Chapter 10 reference.

CAUTION: What is working for us will not necessarily work for you. Only you can decide which systems you are most comfortable with and should only use the results of this workbook as a guide, not the sole basis of your financial plan. It is highly recommended that you seek additional guidance in developing a retirement plan you will be most comfortable with.

Appendix I: Help Creating a Retirement Lifestyle

If you are not yet in retirement and do not have a good understanding of what it will cost to have the lifestyle you want in retirement, the following may help. Remember, you most likely will have more time in retirement to enjoy more activities which may require you to spend more on travel, entertainment, and leisure activities.

Keep in mind that the goal should be to create as flexible a retirement lifestyle as possible, keeping your fixed and necessary expenditures as low as possible to allow for more discretionary spending when your portfolio performs well or to reduce discretionary spending when your portfolio performs poorly in any given year.

Your home: Where will you live? Changing your housing or moving can increase or decrease your expenses. Even if you plan to remain in the same house, some of your costs will still change. For example, your utility bills may increase if you spend more time at home. Or they may decrease if you spend more time traveling away from home. As your home ages you may spend more on repairs and maintenance.

Transportation: What does it cost you now? How might it change in retirement?

Food: Will you eat out more often in retirement, or entertain friends and family more often? Will you spend less because you no longer buy lunches or other food items at work?

Clothing and personal care: How much do you spend to dress for work, and will it be less in retirement.

Health and medical expenses: Will you buy insurance to supplement Medicare gaps, or will you be paying for all your health care insurance until you are age 65? Will you join a health club, or cancel a club membership?

Leisure Activities: Now that you may have more time in retirement, will you spend more on Entertainment such as movies, books, theater, or clubs? What about Hobbies or Recreation activities?

Travel: Will you increase your travel during retirement? Take those bucket list trips?

Income Taxes: After you stop working you will be responsible for withholding taxes on income from taxable accounts and other sources of income from 401K or IRA accounts and capital gains that you do not have income tax withheld. Some of your Social Security Benefits most likely will be taxed. You may be required to make estimated quarterly tax payments, so it is a good idea to review possible future tax implications that reduce spendable income.

Appendix II:

TABLE 5A: Historical Financial Data

Time Period	Cash	Stock % / Bond %						
		0/100	20/80	40/60	50/50	60/40	80/20	100/0
40 Years (1979-2018)								
Average annual gain:	4.5%	7.5%	8.6%	9.6%	10.2%	10.7%	11.7%	12.8%
Worst 1 year:	0.1%	-2.9%	-3.2%	-11.7%	-15.9%	-20.1%	-28.6%	-37.0%
Best 1 year:	14.3%	32.7%	30.4%	28.2%	28.0%	29.9%	29.8%	37.6%
% Years Positive:	100%	90%	93%	90%	88%	83%	83%	83%
92 Years (1926-2017)								
Average annual gain:	3.4%	5.4%	6.7%	7.8%	8.4%	8.8%	9.6%	10.3%
Worst 1 year:	0.0%	-8.1%	-10.1%	-18.4%	-22.5%	-26.6%	-34.9%	-43.1%
Best 1 year:	14.3%	32.6%	29.8%	27.9%	32.3%	36.7%	45.4%	54.2%
% Years Positive:	100%	85%	87%	85%	82%	78%	75%	73%

Average Annual Inflation from 1968 to 2017:

30 Years (1988-2017)   2.6%
35 Years (1983-2017)   2.7%
40 Years (1978-2017)   3.6%
45 Years (1973-2017)   4.0%
50 Years (1968-2017)   4.1%

Cash = 3 month T- bills, Bonds = Barclays U.S. Aggregate Bond index or equivalent
Stocks = SP 500 or equivalent
Source: Vanguard, Morningstar, Author

- 78 -

TABLE 5B: Annual Savings Withdrawal Rates Comparison

Years Left	4% System	1/N System	VPW Stock to Bond ratio				RMD System	
			20/80	40/60	60/40	80/20	Age	%
38	3.40%	2.63%	4.00%	4.40%	4.80%	5.20%	62	2.96%
37	3.46%	2.70%	4.00%	4.40%	4.90%	5.30%	63	3.04%
36	3.54%	2.78%	4.10%	4.50%	4.90%	5.30%	64	3.13%
35	3.61%	2.86%	4.20%	4.60%	5.00%	5.40%	65	3.22%
34	3.70%	2.94%	4.30%	4.70%	5.10%	5.50%	66	3.31%
33	3.78%	3.03%	4.40%	4.70%	5.20%	5.60%	67	3.42%
32	3.88%	3.13%	4.50%	4.80%	5.30%	5.60%	68	3.53%
31	3.97%	3.23%	4.60%	4.90%	5.40%	5.70%	69	3.65%
30	4.08%	3.33%	4.70%	5.00%	5.50%	5.80%	70	3.77%
29	4.19%	3.45%	4.80%	5.10%	5.60%	5.90%	71	3.91%
28	4.31%	3.57%	4.90%	5.20%	5.70%	6.00%	72	4.05%
27	4.44%	3.70%	5.00%	5.40%	5.80%	6.10%	73	4.20%
26	4.58%	3.85%	5.10%	5.50%	5.90%	6.30%	74	4.37%
25	4.73%	4.00%	5.30%	5.60%	6.10%	6.40%	75	4.55%
24	4.90%	4.17%	5.50%	5.80%	6.20%	6.50%	76	4.72%
23	5.07%	4.35%	5.60%	6.00%	6.40%	6.70%	77	4.93%
22	5.27%	4.55%	5.80%	6.10%	6.60%	6.90%	78	5.13%
21	5.48%	4.76%	6.00%	6.40%	6.80%	7.10%	79	5.35%
20	5.72%	5.00%	6.30%	6.60%	7.00%	7.30%	80	5.59%
19	5.98%	5.26%	6.50%	6.80%	7.20%	7.50%	81	5.85%
18	6.27%	5.56%	6.80%	7.10%	7.50%	7.80%	82	6.13%
17	6.59%	5.88%	7.10%	7.40%	7.80%	8.10%	83	6.45%
16	6.95%	6.25%	7.50%	7.80%	8.20%	8.50%	84	6.76%
15	7.36%	6.67%	7.90%	8.20%	8.60%	8.90%	85	7.09%
14	7.84%	7.14%	8.30%	8.60%	9.00%	9.30%	86	7.46%
13	8.38%	7.69%	8.90%	9.20%	9.60%	9.80%	87	7.87%
12	9.01%	8.33%	9.50%	9.80%	10.20%	10.40%	88	8.33%
11	9.77%	9.09%	10.30%	10.50%	10.90%	11.20%	89	8.77%
10	10.67%	10.00%	11.10%	11.40%	11.80%	12.00%	90	9.26%
9	11.77%	11.11%	12.20%	12.50%	12.90%	13.10%	91	9.80%
8	13.15%	12.50%	13.60%	13.90%	14.20%	14.50%	92	10.42%
7	14.92%	14.29%	15.40%	15.60%	16.00%	16.20%	93	10.99%
6	17.29%	16.67%	17.70%	18.00%	18.30%	18.50%	94	11.63%
5	20.60%	20.00%	21.00%	21.20%	21.50%	21.80%	95	12.35%
4	25.57%	25.00%	25.90%	26.20%	26.40%	26.60%	96	13.16%
3	33.86%	33.33%	34.20%	34.40%	34.60%	34.80%	97	14.08%
2	50.46%	50.00%	50.60%	50.80%	50.90%	51.10%	98	14.93%
1	100.0%	100.0%	100.0%	100.0%	100.0%	100.0%	99	15.87%

The VPW table is based on a table Collaboratively developed
by a group of Bogleheads®. www.bogleheads.org

Appendix III: How Am I Doing?

Optional but highly recommended that you use the following form to track your progress over time. This will help you see how well your plan is performing and what adjustments you may need to make.

	At the beginning of each year record amounts from last years totals					
Year	Estimated Annual Income	Actual Annual Income	Estimated Annual Expenses	Actual Annual Expenses	Portfolio Value at End of Previous Year	Change from Previous Year

Appendix IV: A Financial Checklist & To Do List

At the Beginning of Every Year:

If you are using the 4% withdrawal system, take the amount you withdrew last year and increase it by last year's inflation rate. You then add the expected after-tax income for the current year to arrive at your spending budget for the current year.

For the other withdrawal systems, create the current year Desired Spending Budget (Worksheet 1), Expected After-Tax Annual Income (Worksheet 2), and update the Total Spendable Value of Your Portfolio (Worksheet 3) as of the previous December 31. Also fill out the appropriate withdrawal worksheet to determine the suggested withdrawal amount for the current year. I also recommend adding last year's results to the "How Am I Doing" form in Appendix III.

If you or your spouse have tax differed accounts like IRA's and 401K's (Not Roth IRA's) you may be required by the IRS to withdraw a minimum amount based on your age to avoid a 50% penalty being assessed by the IRS for not withdrawing enough. If you are required to withdraw the RMD within the current year, you will need to calculate the amount at the beginning of the year and this amount will be subject to income taxes. You do not have to spend this amount, but you should subtract this amount from the suggested withdrawal amount to determine if you must withdraw more from your savings to meet your spending needs. (See Chapter 8 on which accounts to withdraw from and in what order).

After You have determined your withdrawal amount:

Now that you know your withdrawal amount for the year, you will need to decide when to withdraw it and which accounts to withdraw from. You will also need to determine if quarterly estimated income tax payments will be required and when to pay them.

It may also be a good time to check your portfolio to see if further re-balancing is necessary to maintain your target stock, bond and cash ratios. See Chapters 8 & 9 for further advice.

Mid-Year: Review your income and spending budget to see how you are doing and if spending adjustments need to be made.

Near the End of the Year: It is a good time to review how your plan is doing and begin preparing for the beginning of next year when you start the above process over again.

Appendix V: References & Resources

Chapter 8 reference:

www.caniretireyet.com is a good retirement resource. One of the many articles on the site discusses the importance of where you should withdraw your money from based on stock and bond market performance to maximize your investment gains over time. See the article "The Best Retirement Withdrawal Strategies: Digging Deeper" by Darrow Kirkpatrick.

Chapter 9 reference:

"Determinants of Portfolio Performance" by Gary P. Brinson, L. Rudolph Hood, and Gilbert L. Beebower

www.morningstar.com Christine Benz has several good articles on the basics of setting up and maintaining a "Bucket" retirement portfolio, including some of her favorite funds for retirees.

Chapter 10 reference:

For more information regarding the VPW withdrawal system and inflation-indexed Single Premium Immediate Annuity or SPIA, go to **www.bogleheads.org.** It is also a great source for investing and retirement information.

Additional Resources:

www.Vanguard.com and **www.Fidelity.com** are excellent resources regarding retirement planning.

"Common Sense on Mutual Funds" John C. Bogle founder of Vanguard

"How much can I spend in retirement? A guide to investment-based retirement income strategies" a book written by Wade Pfau Ph.D., CFA is an excellent reference book although quite lengthy with lots of detail.

"The Bogleheads' Guide to Retirement Planning" a book by Taylor Larimore, Mel Lindauer, Richard A. Ferri, and Laura F. Dogu

"The 4% Rule Safe Withdrawal rates in Retirement" a book by Todd Tresidder

"Asset Dedication: How to grow Wealthy with The Next Generation of Asset Allocation" a book by Stephen J. Huxley and J. Brent Burns

Afterword

The free companion spreadsheet to this workbook is available both as a Microsoft Excel .xlsx and as a LibreOffice .ods. To receive it, send me an email at **spendmore2019@outlook.com** and let me know which version you want.

If you would rather receive printable copies of the worksheets to fill in manually, send me an email request for the Worksheets pdf file.

If this workbook helped you answer the questions raised at the beginning of the workbook and that it was worth reading, please let others know by providing a review at **www.amazon.com**. Search on my workbook title or my name then scroll down until you see "Write a Customer Review" and click on it. Reviews truly matter in helping others discover my book and I read every one of them.

You might be interested in my new book "**Solving a Retirement Dilemma – *Spend Less or Run Out of Money***" - How to Spend More – Live the Lifestyle You deserve – Make it last a Lifetime. Unlike this step by step workbook, it is a book that allowed me to significantly expand on the many retirement issues and decisions we faced along with the successes, failures, and mistakes we made in planning for and living in retirement.

If you were not satisfied, or you have suggestions for making this workbook better, please let me know and I promise I will respond.

Thank you for purchasing this workbook.

Made in the USA
Monee, IL
03 September 2021